1980

The Year I Was Born

Compiled by Sally Tagholm

Illustrated by Michael Evans

FANTAIL

in association with Signpost Books

FANTAIL PUBLISHING, AN IMPRINT OF PUFFIN ENTERPRISES
Published by the Penguin Group
Penguin Books Ltd, 27 Wrights Lane, London W8 5TZ, England
Penguin Books USA Inc., 375 Hudson Street, New York, NY 10014, USA
Penguin Books Australia Ltd., Ringwood, Victoria, Australia
Penguin Books Canada Ltd, 10 Alcorn Avenue, Toronto, Ontario, Canada
M4V 3B2
Penguin Books (NZ) Ltd, 182–190 Wairau Road, Auckland 10, New Zealand

Penguin Books Ltd., Registered Offices: Harmondsworth, Middlesex,
England

First published 1991
Published by Penguin Books in association with Signpost Books
10 9 8 7 6 5

Based on an original idea by Sally Wood
Conceived, designed and produced by Signpost Books Ltd, 1991
Copyright in this format © 1991 Signpost Books Ltd.,
25 Eden Drive, Headington, Oxford OX3 0AB, England

Illustrations copyright © 1991 Michael Evans
Text copyright © 1991 Sally Tagholm

Editor: Dorothy Wood
Art Director: Treld Bicknell
Paste up: Naomi Games

ISBN 1 874785 00 7 Hardback edition
ISBN 0140 90332 1 Paperback edition

Colour separations by Fotographics, Ltd.
Printed and bound in Belgium by Proost Book Production through
Landmark Production Consultants, Ltd.

Typeset by DP Photosetting, Aylesbury, Bucks

ME

Name: Leanne Naysmith
Date of birth: 2/10/80
Time of birth: 11·07 pm
Place of birth: Dunfermline
Weight at birth: 9½ lbs
Colour of eyes: Blue → brown
Colour of hair (if any): Black
Distinguishing marks:

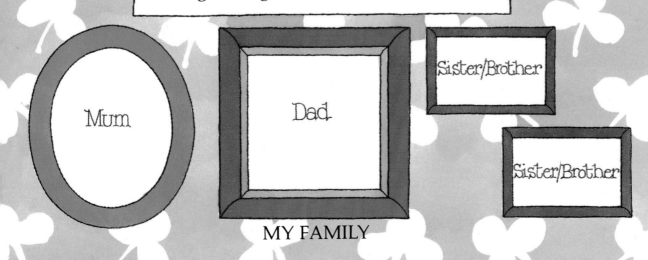

Mum

Dad

Sister/Brother

Sister/Brother

MY FAMILY

January

Tuesday *January 1*	Bank Holiday. Earthquake measuring 6.9 on the Richter Scale in the Azores, and an earth tremor measuring 3 in the Scottish borders.
Wednesday *January 2*	49th Model Engineer Exhibition opens at Wembley Conference Centre in London. Full Moon −13°C at Stoke-on-Trent
Thursday *January 3*	Tea and shredded suet are going metric: ¼ lb packs become 125 grams and ½ lb packs 250 grams.
Friday *January 4*	The Transglobe Expedition, which set off from Greenwich on September 2, 1979, reaches Antarctica.
Saturday *January 5*	A giant oil slick along the Cornish coast. Hundreds of injured birds are taken to a special RSPCA sanctuary nr Taunton, Somerset.
Sunday *January 6*	Good weather for toadstools like saffron milk caps (*lactarius deliciosus*), horns of plenty (*craterellus cornucopoides*), fairy ring champignons (*marasmius oreades*) and blewitts (*lepista saevium*). Mrs Indira Gandhi is elected Prime Minister of India.
Monday *January 7*	Hundreds of telephones are out of order in Cheltenham because rats have gnawed through the underground cables. Snowploughs out in Sussex.
Tuesday *January 8*	A 12-seater Sikorsky helicopter makes a record round-trip flight: London–Paris 75mins; Paris–London 71mins.
Wednesday *January 9*	Alain Cattienneau (Fr) is voted Yachtsman of the Year. He rescued the crew of the British yacht *Griffin* during the Fastnet race last year.
Thursday *January 10*	Lt-Col John Blashford-Snell returns from Operation Drake. He reports the sighting of a Salvadori Dragon lizard nearly 5.5m long off the Gulf of Papua, New Guinea.
Friday *January 11*	Nigel Short (14), from Bolton, becomes the youngest ever International Chess Master at the Hastings Tournament.
Saturday *January 12*	A large statue of Charlie Chaplin is found in Leicester Square. It is taken to Bow Street Police Station. A small earth tremor in Gwent, South Wales, at 8.50am.
Sunday *January 13*	St Hilary's Day. Tiddlywink, a female Brown Bear cub, is born at London Zoo. She weighs 0.68kg.
Monday *January 14*	Snow, freezing rain, black ice and fog in England and Wales. It's so cold that the sea freezes at Pegwell Bay, nr Ramsgate, Kent!

January

Named after the Roman god, Janus, who had two faces and could look backwards and forwards at the same time. Also known as 'frosty-month', 'after-yule', 'first-month' and 'snow-month'.

OPERATION DRAKE

Operation Drake celebrates the 400th anniversary of Sir Francis Drake's famous voyage (1577–1580) round the world in the *Golden Hind*. The expedition set off in October 1978 in a 150-tonne sailing ship called *Eye of the Wind*. It is equipped with a special science laboratory and is following Drake's original route. In Papua, New Guinea, they discovered a snake with no eyes (and pimples instead of scales), and sea-faring crocodiles over 10m long—as well as monster lizards!

THE TRANSGLOBE EXPEDITION

The British Transglobe Expedition left England in September 1979 to circumnavigate the globe via the south and north poles. This January, the team are setting up base camp at Ryvingen in Antarctica, where they are spending the long, dark polar winter in temperatures as low as –50°C.

Robert Burns, Scotland's most famous poet, was born on January 25, 1759. Scots all over the world celebrate his birthday by eating haggis, which in a poem Burns called 'Great Chieftain o'the pudden race'. Here is what the dictionary says: Haggis (hae.gis) a dish consisting of the heart, lungs and liver of a sheep, calf etc, minced with suet and oatmeal, seasoned with salt, pepper, onions etc and boiled like a large sausage in the maw* of the animal. (A popular English dish till the 18th century but now considered peculiarly Scottish.)

* stomach

Blag ★
NATIONAL STEEL STRIKE BEGINS

The Daily Scoop
NATURALIST JOY ADAMSON, AUTHOR OF *BORN FREE*, KILLED IN KENYA

CHIT-CHAT
MRS GHANDI WINS GENERAL ELECTION IN INDIA

The Reporter
DR. ANDREI SAKHAROV AND WIFE EXILED FROM MOSCOW

Tuesday *January 15*	The 3-man Transglobe team say goodbye to their support ship *Benjamin Bowring* and start preparing for their long journey across Antarctica.
Wednesday *January 16*	Mr D.H.F. Somerset is the new Chief Cashier at the Bank of England. His signature will appear on all new bank notes.
Thursday *January 17*	The *Discovery*, which took Captain Scott and his crew on the first British Antarctic Expedition 1901–1904, is moved from the Embankment in London to Sheerness for repairs. New Moon
Friday *January 18*	Blood samples from Devonport Hospital, Plymouth are being flown by racing pigeon to the Central Blood Bank Laboratory. It's quick and very cheap—only £1 a week in birdseed!
Saturday *January 19*	The northbound carriageway of the M1 motorway is blocked for 6 hrs when a lorry carrying 20 tonnes of grapefruit overturns.
Sunday *January 20*	Avalanches at Sca Fell and Helvellyn in the Lake District. Giant Japanese seaweed is spreading along the coast of Sussex.
Monday *January 21*	Concorde is 4! Very heavy snowfall. 100 pigs are stranded in a snowdrift 1.2m deep between Birdsall and Leavening, nr Malton, Yorkshire.
Tuesday *January 22*	A Greek freighter, the *Athina B*, runs aground near the Palace Pier, Brighton, carrying a cargo of pumice worth £45,000.
Wednesday *January 23*	Jimmy Savile launches an appeal to rebuild the Spinal Injury Centre at Stoke Mandeville Hospital in Buckinghamshire. Each brick costs £5!
Thursday *January 24*	Robin Cousins wins a gold medal at the European Figure Skating Championships, Goteborg. Earthquake in San Francisco measures 5.5 on the Richter Scale.
Friday *January 25*	Burns' Night: in Glasgow they celebrate with a monster haggis 1.5m long and nearly 1m wide, which is packed into 7 ox stomachs sewn together.
Saturday *January 26*	Australia Day. The Mont Blanc tunnel from France to Italy is open again after being closed by avalanches.
Sunday *January 27*	Hurricane Hyacinth devastates the island of Réunion in the Pacific. Space Lego is the Toy of the Year.

Monday *January 28*	James Irwin, the American astronaut who landed on the Moon on the Apollo 15 mission in 1972, starts a lecture tour of British schools. A deadly 10cm Jockey Spider is found in some bananas in Stevenage, Hertfordshire.
Tuesday *January 29*	A plague of starlings is destroying the crops in Brittany. Farmers have tried letting off fireworks and dropping chemical jelly bombs to scare them away but nothing has worked!
Wednesday *January 30*	The Olympic Flame is kindled at Olympia in Greece, and starts on its way to the 13th Winter Olympic Games at Lake Placid, New York, USA.
Thursday *January 31*	21 plastic decoy geese are in use at Thorney Island, Sussex to lure Brent Geese away from the winter corn crops by the shores of Chichester Harbour.

The British Family 1980

Mr and Mrs 1980 and the little 1980s spend, on average, £7.21 each on food a week. They each drink 4.16 pints of milk a week and eat 110.3 grams of cheese; 476.3 grams of red meat; 135.1 grams of fish; 3.69 eggs each; 317.5 grams of sugar; 1kg 162 grams of potatoes; 589.7 grams of fresh fruit; 881.7 grams of bread; 114.9 grams of biscuits (plain); 31.7 grams of biscuits (chocolate), 69.2 grams of ice cream for pudding; 9.1 grams of jelly and drink 0.62 litres of soft drinks.

WEEKLY SHOPPING BILL FOR ONE

Milk and cream	77.33p
Cheese	21.99p
Meat	185.99p
Fish	25.62p
Eggs	16.13p
Sugar	12.86p
Veg	74.03p
Fresh fruit	38.72p
Bread	37.99p
Biscuits	21.41p
Breakfast cereals	11.20p
Tea	7.60p
Coffee	11.74p
Cocoa/drinking choc	0.81p

Total £5.43

(These figures are taken from the National Food Survey)

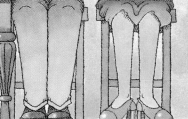

February

Friday **February 1**	A cyclone races along the NW coast of Australia with winds of 200kph. *The Times* crossword is 50 years old. Full Moon
Saturday **February 2**	The Assistant Masters and Mistresses Association publishes a report saying that parents do not talk to their children enough.
Sunday **February 3**	An earthquake measuring 6.3 on the Richter Scale in the Pacific islands of Samoa. *Odin's Raven*, the replica of a Viking longship, appears in front of the British Museum in London for the new Viking Exhibition.
Monday **February 4**	School meals go up by 5p to 35p from today. Stamps go up by 2p—1st class to 12p and 2nd class to 10p.
Tuesday **February 5**	Jean-Marc Boivin receives the International Award for Valour in Sport at the Guildhall, London. He hang-glided down K2 in the Himalayas, the second highest mountain in the world in 13mins.
Wednesday **February 6**	Mrs Thatcher is made freeman of the Borough of Barnet, which includes her own constituency, Finchley.
Thursday **February 7**	The Duke of Wellington plants a 30cm Turkey Oak tree at London Zoo. It was grown from an acorn from the tree planted by the grave of 'Copenhagen', the horse ridden by the first duke at the Battle of Waterloo.
Friday **February 8**	Tonnes of mackerel fall off a lorry on the M5 and close 8km of the motorway between Taunton and Wellington, Somerset, for 4hrs.
Saturday **February 9**	Champion Shargleam Blackcap, a 2½-year-old flat-coated retriever, wins the Best in Show title at Crufts Dog Show, Earls Court, London.
Sunday **February 10**	Photographs from the Voyager 2 spacecraft show that the planet Jupiter has a 14th moon which is only 40km in diameter. Its orbital 'year' is only 7hrs 8mins!
Monday **February 11**	British Rail introduce games trains on their London–Northampton service. Games like Draughts and Roads and Rails (a version of Snakes and Ladders) are printed on the tables.
Tuesday **February 12**	The Winter Olympics open at Lake Placid, USA. St Clement Danes (the church in the nursery rhyme 'Oranges and Lemons') gets a new tenor bell.
Wednesday **February 13**	A Royal Proclamation calls in all sixpences (2½ pence pieces). They will not be legal tender after June 30.

Thursday February 14	St Valentine's Day. Solar Max, the first satellite to study solar flares, goes into orbit round the earth.
Friday February 15	Two dead whales are washed up on the beaches at Southsea in Hampshire and Hastings in Sussex.

February

The Roman month of purification. The name comes from the Latin 'februo' which means 'I purify by sacrifice'. It has also been known as 'sprout kale' and 'rain month'.

Leap Year

Most years have 365 days; Leap Years are special because they have 366. The extra day is added once every four years to even things up with the solar year of 365.242 days—that's the exact time it takes the earth to go round the sun. The extra day is always added on to the end of February, which normally has 28 days, but in a Leap Year has 29.

The XIII Winter Olympics at Lake Placid, NY State, USA

1,283 competitors from 38 countries take part in the Games.
East Germany wins 23 medals (9 gold)
USSR wins 22 medals (10 gold)
USA wins 12 medals (6 gold)

The star of the Games is the US ice speed skater Eric Heiden (21), who wins 5 gold medals, winning every event in his sport.

Trumpet
FRENCH FARMERS ON STILTS DEMONSTRATE AGAINST BRITISH SHEEP

The Herald
BR ISSUE EMERGENCY HAMPERS THEY CONTAIN BLANKETS, BOVRIL AND MARS BARS

Gossip
CHRISTMAS MESSAGE BROADCAST BY MISTAKE ON BBC RADIO 4'S 'PRAYER FOR TODAY'

Daily Bleet
BARK POWER! THERE ARE 1000 MORE DOGS AT CRUFTS THIS YEAR

Saturday *February 16*	Chinese New Year—it's the beginning of the Year of the Monkey! New Moon
Sunday *February 17*	The *Athina B*, which ran aground on Brighton beach in January, is finally refloated. The Salvation Army plays 'Rule Britannia'.
Monday *February 18*	More than 150 spectators at the Winter Olympics at Lake Placid are treated for frostbite, in temperatures of –10°C.
Tuesday *February 19*	Pancake Day. Liberal, Kansas, USA, beats Olney, Bucks, UK, in the annual Pancake Race. Liberal cover the 379m course in 1min 03.55secs!
Wednesday *February 20*	The French Government withdraws silver 5 franc, 10 franc and 50 franc coins from circulation. They've got too much silver in them. (The silver content of the 5 franc piece is worth about 45 francs!)
Thursday *February 21*	Robin Cousins wins Britain's only gold medal at the Winter Olympics—for figure skating. A cheque, signed in 1795 by Lord Nelson with his right hand, which he later lost in battle, is sold for £600 at Stanley Gibbons in London.
Friday *February 22*	A Saxon skeleton, more than 900 years old, is dug up by workmen at Cranworth, Norfolk.
Saturday *February 23*	Berkshire County Council approves a new by-law prohibiting sleeping in libraries: fine £20.
Sunday *February 24*	Watch out for new Toad Warning signs on the A40 at Dowdeswell, Cheltenham, Glos. Last year, hundreds of toads were killed crossing the road to breed in the reservoir.
Monday *February 25*	The Right Reverend Robert Runcie is confirmed as the 102nd Archbishop of Canterbury and Primate of All England.
Tuesday *February 26*	A Royal Navy minesweeper sinks dozens of drums of ammonia floating off the Lizard, Cornwall.
Wednesday *February 27*	A service of thanksgiving is held in St Paul's Cathedral for Sir Barnes Wallis (92), who died last October. He invented the bouncing bomb used by the 'Dam Busters' in World War II.
Thursday *February 28*	A Leap Frogging Contest in London launches Leap Frog Year, in aid of St John's Ambulance.
Friday *February 29*	Leap Year's Day: if you are born today, you'll only have a birthday once every four years!

UK Fact File 1980

Olympic Year

February 29th Leap Year

Total area of the United Kingdom
244,090 sq kms

Capital City
London
(1580 sq kms
population 6,877,000)

Population of UK

55,945,000
(Approximately 106
females for each 100
males)

Average population per sq km   229

Births | 754,000 | Marriages | 414,000 | Deaths | 661,000 |

Most popular girls' name*

Elizabeth   James

Most popular boys' name*

Licensed vehicles
19,200,000

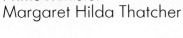

Head of State
Queen Elizabeth II

Prime Minister
Margaret Hilda Thatcher

Astronomer Royal
Sir Martin Ryle

Poet Laureate
Sir John Betjeman

Poetry

Archibishop of Canterbury
Frederick Donald
Coggan (until March)
Robert Alexander
Kennedy Runcie

President of
European Parliament
Simone Veil

Members of Parliament
635 (19 are women)

President of European Commission
Roy Jenkins

Members of EEC
Belgium,
Denmark,

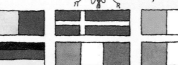

France, Federal Republic
of Germany, Ireland,
Italy, Luxembourg, the
Netherlands, UK

* according to *The Times* newspaper

March

Saturday March 1
St David's Day. The Duchess of Gloucester has a baby girl at St Mary's Hospital, London. She weighs nearly 3.8kg, and will be called Rose Victoria Brigitte Louise.

Full Moon

Sunday March 2
Betty, a 20-year-old giant Indian Hornbill, who lives at Birdland in Bourton-on-the-Water, Glos. has had a new acrylic beak fitted after losing her old one because of faulty blood vessels.

Monday March 3
Lancelot, the Bewick's Swan, and his mate Elaine, leave the Wildfowl Trust at Slimbridge, Glos. to fly to their breeding grounds in the Arctic. It's his 17th winter in Slimbridge.

Tuesday March 4
The Forth Bridge is 90 years old! The Prince of Wales rides in his first horse race: he comes second on *Long Wharf* at Plumpton.

Wednesday March 5
Dr Malcolm Longair is appointed Astronomer Royal for Scotland. The World Conservation Strategy is launched in London.

Thursday March 6
Goliath, a baby gorilla, is born by Caesarian section to Diana and Sampson at Bristol Zoo. He weighs just over 2kg.

Friday March 7
The tanker *Tanio* breaks in half during heavy storms in the English Channel, spilling about 3,000 tonnes of oil.

Saturday March 8
International Women's Day. Millions of women in China take the day off work.

Sunday March 9
Oil is still leaking from the broken tanker *Tanio* at the rate of 7 tonnes a day—about 9km of Britanny's coastline has been polluted.

Monday March 10
Commonwealth Day. Liverpool's Anglican Cathedral, which was started in 1904, receives an award for sheer excellence and architectural quality from the Royal Institute of British Architects.

Tuesday March 11
Prince Andrew starts a 14-day course at the Royal Marines Training Camp at Lympstone in Devon. He will do a 48km march, a 17km hike in full combat gear, and sleep rough.

Wednesday March 12
The Post Office issues five new stamps to celebrate the 150th anniversary of the Liverpool and Manchester Railway.

Thursday March 13
Robin Cousins wins a silver medal in the World Figure Skating Championships in Germany.

Friday March 14
Ariel V, Britain's first X-ray satellite, which was launched in October 1974 to function for a year, finally stops working.

March

Named after the Roman god Mars. It has also been known as 'rough-month', 'lengthening-month', 'boisterous-month' and 'windy-month'.

Betty's New Beak

Betty's new beak was made at the Eastman Dental Hospital, London. The Giant Indian Hornbill had 6 fittings before the new acrylic plastic beak was glued in place. The beak had to be exactly the right colour (bright yellow), shape and size (25.4cms), so that her mate would welcome her back. The tip is reinforced with steel because she kept breaking the end off.

World Health Warning!

Scientists, conservationists and representatives from over 100 governments have spent more than 3 years preparing the World Conservation Strategy, a detailed report on the environment and the earth's natural resources. It says that by the end of the century, between 500,000 and 1,000,000 species might be extinct. The report warns that tropical rainforests are being cut down at the rate of 110,075 sq kms a year—that's an area about the size of Wales, and this might increase the amount of carbon dioxide in the air and change the world's climate.

Saturday March 15	Wolverhampton Wanderers win the League Cup at Wembley. They beat Nottingham Forest 1-0.
Sunday March 16	British Summer Time starts at 2am. Operation Drake (see Jan 10) begins search for two cannon thrown overboard by Sir Francis Drake off Sulawesi in Indonesia. His ship, the *Golden Hind*, was too heavy with gold and spices! New Moon
Monday March 17	St Patrick's Day. Snow blizzards in the north. The Lake District is badly hit with more than 20cm of snow.
Tuesday March 18	The Royal Research Ship *Discovery* arrives at St Katharine's Docks from Sheerness, where she started her repairs.
Wednesday March 19	More blizzards in the north and north west of England. Gales in the south and Wales. Huge waves crash over the sea wall at Rhos-on-Sea, near Colwyn Bay, and flood the main street.
Thursday March 20	The 274 tonne *Mi Amigo*, the pirate Radio Caroline ship, sinks in a Force 9 gale off Clacton.
Friday March 21	Two sections of the Humber Bridge, which will be the longest single-span suspension bridge in the world when it is completed, collapse and dangle above the ground. They each weigh 125 tonnes!
Saturday March 22	A special 2000th edition of the comic *Dandy* is published today (7p). The very first was published on December 4, 1937.
Sunday March 23	Acres of Ashdown Forest near Nutley, Sussex, are on fire. Women's University Boat Race: Oxford beats Cambridge at Henley by 1½ lengths.
Monday March 24	The island of Guernsey issues a £20 note for the first time. It also issues a new set of £1, £5 and £10 notes.
Tuesday March 25	The Right Reverend Robert Runcie is enthroned in Canterbury Cathedral. He wears a gold mitre and a cape of wild silk, studded with amethyst-coloured beads.
Wednesday March 26	Earth tremors, about 2 on the Richter Scale, in northern Cumbria and southern Scotland. Budget Day: child benefit will go up by 75p in November to £4.75.
Thursday March 27	Mount St Helen's, the volcano in Washington State, USA, erupts for the first time since 1857. Ching Ching, the Giant Panda, has an emergency stomach operation at London Zoo.

Friday *March 28*	6km of ash and gas rise into the sky above the Mount St Helen's volcano. The new Transport Museum opens in the old Flower Market in Covent Garden, London.
Saturday *March 29*	*Ben Nevis* (40-1) wins the Grand National at Aintree. Storm-force winds blow cars off the roads in Devon.
Sunday *March 30*	Mount St Helen's erupts again and a huge new crater opens at the summit. Full Moon—the second this month!
Monday *March 31*	The World Health Organization's NO SMOKING DAY. Jesse Owens (66), who won 4 gold medals at the 1936 Berlin Olympics, dies.

12ᴾ · LIVERPOOL AND MANCHESTER RAILWAY 1830
12ᴾ · LIVERPOOL AND MANCHESTER RAILWAY 1830
12ᴾ · LIVERPOOL AND MANCHESTER RAILWAY 1830
12ᴾ · LIVERPOOL AND MANCHESTER RAILWAY 1830
12ᴾ · LIVERPOOL AND MANCHESTER RAILWAY 1830

March 30: The giant blasts sent plumes of volcanic ash 18,000m into the sky, and molten rocks swept down the mountain and flattened every tree within a 310sq km area.

The Bugle
PRICELESS 8th CENTURY GOLDEN CHALICE FOUND IN CO. TIPPERARY

DAILY CHUCKLE
USA TO BOYCOTT MOSCOW OLYMPICS

Blurb
OIL PLATFORM DISASTER: 'ALEXANDER KIELLAND' CAPSIZES IN NORTH SEA

World News
ELECTRONIC TABLE TENNIS ROBOT HELPS CHINESE PLAYER WITH THEIR SHOTS

April

Tuesday *April 1*	Brighton's first nudist beach opens today. The basic charge for telegrams goes up from 70p to £1. The cost for each word goes up from 7p to 10p.
Wednesday *April 2*	Ching Ching, the Giant Panda, is in a critical condition. She is being fed intravenously with honey, glucose and vitamins.
Thursday *April 3*	The Maundy Service at Worcester Cathedral. The Queen distributes Maundy money to 54 women and 54 men. (The recipients match the Queen's age—she'll be 54 on April 21.)
Friday *April 4*	A state of emergency is declared as Mount St Helen's in Washington State, USA, erupts again.
Saturday *April 5*	Oxford beats Cambridge in the University Boat Race. It's the closest finish ever—apart from the dead heat of 1877. The world's most valuable stamp—a one cent 1856 British Guiana magenta-coloured octagon—is auctioned in New York for £450,000.
Sunday *April 6*	Easter Sunday. Ching Ching has her stitches taken out. 400th anniversary of the London Earthquake.
Monday *April 7*	Ching Ching is getting better. She eats 9 eggs, half a pot of honey, some minced beef, bamboo shoots and some protein pellets.
Tuesday *April 8*	The Duke of Edinburgh plants a new kind of disease-free elm tree in Windsor Great Park.
Wednesday *April 9*	Two Soviet cosmonauts, Leonid Popov and Valery Ryumin, are launched in a Soyuz-35, the first manned space flight for a year.
Thursday *April 10*	The Soviet cosmonauts dock with Salyut-6, the space station which has been in orbit for more than 2½ years.
Friday *April 11*	The Long Man of Wilmington, on the Sussex Downs nr Eastbourne, get his turf trimmed by the National Conservation Corps.
Saturday *April 12*	More than 16 hectares of woodland at Buxted Heath in Norfolk are destroyed by fire.
Sunday *April 13*	The first boxing tournament takes place in China since 1959, when it was condemned as decadent.
Monday *April 14*	A lump of ice falls out of the sky from an aeroplane in Lyndhurst, Hampshire.

21°C in eastern England—the hottest day of the year so far.

April

The opening month—from the Latin 'aperire' which means to open. Also known as the time of budding.

Ching Ching, the Giant Panda, and her partner Chia Chia were given to Prime Minister Edward Heath in 1974 when he visited China. Their names mean Crystal Bright and Most Excellent. Ching Ching has her stomach operation in the Animal Hospital at London Zoo, where they treat about 500 patients each year. Ching Ching's operation lasts 3 hours and she has 30 stitches in her stomach. While she is convalescing she gets sacks of get-well cards and telegrams!

EARTHQUAKE

There have been more than 40 earthquakes in Britain in the last thousand years—particularly in south-east England. There was one in Colchester in 1884, one in London in 1580 and one in Lincoln in 1185. In the London Earthquake on April 6, 1580, Westminster Abbey, St Paul's Cathedral and the Temple Church were slightly damaged and 2 people were killed by stones falling from the roof of Christ's Church, Newgate. Although it is known as the London Earthquake, the epicentre was probably in the Straits of Dover and it shook lots of southern England, northern France and the Low Countries. Part of the white cliffs at Dover collapsed and a bit of Dover Castle fell into the sea.

April 9
The Post Office issues a new 50 pence stamp to celebrate the London 1980 International Stamp Exhibition.

London 1980 50P

INTERNATIONAL STAMP EXHIBITION

Tuesday *April 15*	The McDonalds Hamburger chain was founded in the USA 25 years ago. The Tree Council launches a campaign to plant 60,000,000 trees in Britain. Mount Etna in Sicily rumbles. New Moon
Wednesday *April 16*	Glasgow's new underground system starts today—complete with 33 new orange trains.
Thursday *April 17*	Britain's last African colony, Rhodesia, gains its independence at midnight. It is renamed Zimbabwe and becomes the 43rd member of the Commonwealth.
Friday *April 18*	British Rail's new Advanced Passenger Train jumps tracks at 160kph during trials nr Carnforth in Lancashire.
Saturday *April 19*	A new pair of osprey arrive at the RSPB's sanctuary at Loch Garten, Speyside. They have flown all the way from West Africa.
Sunday *April 20*	Force 10 and 11 gales hit the south and east coasts of England. The sea fronts at Margate, Ramsgate and Broadstairs are badly damaged. Nicholas Daniel (18) from Winchester, who plays the oboe, wins the BBC Young Musician of the Year title.
Monday *April 21*	The Queen is 54 today. She celebrates her birthday at Windsor Castle.
Tuesday *April 22*	Stephenson's *Rocket* leaves the Science Museum in London for the first time in 120 years to join in the celebrations of the 150th anniversary of the Liverpool and Manchester Railway.
Wednesday *April 23*	David Scott Couper returns to Plymouth in his yacht *Ocean Bound*, having sailed single-handed round the world in 248 days.
Thursday *April 24*	Gloucestershire is declared an official drought zone after three weeks without rain.
Friday *April 25*	Fagging at Eton College is to be abolished at the end of this term.
Saturday *April 26*	The Soviet Union launches an unmanned Progress-9 spaceship to take supplies to the two cosmonauts on board the orbiting Salyut-6 space station.
Sunday *April 27*	Two osprey eggs are laid at Loch Garten, Speyside. The former Clyde paddle steamer *Old Caledonia*, which is moored near Waterloo Bridge in London, catches fire.

Monday *April 28*	Two lionesses called Jessie and Girlie escape from a circus and leap into a school in Devizes, Wilts, at lunchtime.
Tuesday *April 29*	Sir Alfred Hitchcock, who made *Psycho* and lots of other frightening films, dies today.
Wednesday *April 30*	The Metrication Board, which was set up in 1969 to help change pounds into kilos and yards into metres, is abolished. Last day for exchanging silver 5 franc, 10 franc and 50 franc coins in France! Full Moon

Nobody quite knows who the Long Man of Wilmington is, where he came from, or how old he is. He could be about 700yrs, or almost 3000!

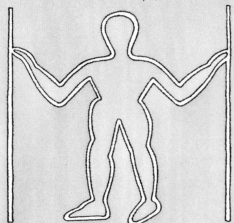

He is more than 70m tall and just over 36m wide, and probably the biggest representation of a human being anywhere in the world.

The Owl

DR CANAAN BANANA IS MADE FIRST PRESIDENT OF ZIMBABWE

Daily Sensation

QUEEN IS GIVEN LARGE CHOCOLATE CHALET IN SWITZERLAND

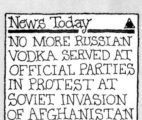

News Today

NO MORE RUSSIAN VODKA SERVED AT OFFICIAL PARTIES IN PROTEST AT SOVIET INVASION OF AFGHANISTAN

Town Crier

QUEEN JULIANA OF THE NETHERLANDS ABDICATES

Anniversaries 1980

Real Tennis is 450 years old
Liverpool to Manchester Railway is 150 years old
Royal Geographical Society is 150 years old
The *Daily Telegraph* is 125 years old
Guildhall School of Music and Drama is 100 years old
Welsh Rugby Union is 100 years old
Institute of Chartered Accountants is 100 years old
Jersey Royal Fluke Potato is 100 years old
Amateur Athletics Association is 100 years old
Amateur Boxing Association is 100 years old
Automobile Association is 75 years old
Popeye is 50 years old
The Times Crossword is 50 years old
Independent Television is 25 years old
Concorde is 4 years old

May

Thursday *May 1*	A new permanent exhibition, 'Man's Place in Evolution', opens at the Natural History Museum in London.
Friday *May 2*	There are more tremors inside Mount Etna, Sicily, as lava builds up inside a new crater on the south west slope.
Saturday *May 3*	Start of celebrations to mark the 150th anniversary of the Canterbury to Whitstable Railway.
Sunday *May 4*	80 miners take part in the Flitton Potato Race in Bedfordshire. They each have to carry a sack of potatoes that weighs nearly 25.5kg for 1.5km.
Monday *May 5*	Bank Holiday. Croydon Aerodrome is re-opened today to celebrate the 50th anniversary of Amy Johnson's solo flight to Australia. It took her 19 days to fly the 19,380km in her second-hand Gypsy Moth bi-plane *Jason*.
Tuesday *May 6*	Three new stamps are issued in Jersey to celebrate 100 years of the Jersey Royal potato. International Stamp Exhibition opens at Earls Court in London.
Wednesday *May 7*	Scientists at the Jet Propulsion Laboratory in Pasadena identify a 15th moon orbiting Jupiter from photographs sent back from *Voyager 1*.
Thursday *May 8*	The 33rd World Health Assembly in Geneva declares that the world is free from smallpox.
Friday *May 9*	The Archbishop of Canterbury and the Pope have a breakfast meeting in Accra, West Africa. Beginning of a long spell of unbroken sunshine in the eastern half of England.
Saturday *May 10*	West Ham wins the FA Cup Final at Wembley: they beat Arsenal 1-0. Celebrations start in Plymouth to mark the 400th anniversary of Sir Francis Drake's voyage round the world.
Sunday *May 11*	Peter Dowdeswell (40) from Northamptonshire, eats 153 prunes in 47 seconds to claim his 145th world record.
Monday *May 12*	An international team of scientists and conservationists sets out from Peking to rescue pandas and find ways of protecting them.
Tuesday *May 13*	Hosepipe ban in Devon and parts of Cornwall. There has been no rain for more than a month. The sunniest spring for at least 100 years in Glasgow.

May

Takes its name from Maia, the goddess of growth and increase, or from 'maiores', the Latin word for elders, who were honoured this month.
The Anglo Saxons called it 'thrimilce' because cows could be milked three times a day now.
An old Dutch name was 'bloumaand' which means blossoming month.

VENUS OBSERVED

Apart from the Maxwell Mountains*, everything on the planet Venus is named after women. There are goddesses and heroines galore. You'll find highlands called Aphrodite and Ishtar, and valleys called Hecate and Diana, Eve, Cleopatra, Pavlova, Colette and Nightingale!

* Named after a famous scientist called James Clerk Maxwell (1831–1879)

The Royal Jersey Fluke Potato

The Royal Jersey Fluke Potato was born by chance 100 years ago. A Jersey farmer, Hugh de la Haye gave a grand dinner for his neighbours. After they had finished eating, he cut an ordinary round potato into 15 pieces, each piece with an eye in it, and planted them in a nearby valley. The following spring a huge and very early crop of small, kidney-shaped potatoes was produced. And that's how it became known as the Royal Jersey Fluke!

7p JERSEY — *Centenary of the Jersey Royal* — R. Granger-Barrett 1980 Questa

15p JERSEY — *Centenary of the Jersey Royal* — R. Granger-Barrett 1980 Questa

17½p JERSEY — *Centenary of the Jersey Royal* — R. Granger-Barrett 1980 Questa

Grapevine
SAS STORM IRANIAN EMBASSY IN LONDON AND RESCUE HOSTAGES

Good Egg
LORD NELSON GETS CLEAN-UP IN TRAFALGAR SQUARE

Chatterbox
APPLE WAR HOTS UP – THE COX'S ORANGE PIPPIN VERSUS THE FRENCH GOLDEN DELICIOUS

Newsreel
ISLAND OF JERSEY HOLDS DINNER IN HONOUR OF THE JERSEY ROYAL FLUKE POTATO

Wednesday *May 14*	A Spanish expedition conquers Everest. They're the 22nd team to get to the top since Hillary and Tenzing first climbed it in 1953. New Moon
Thursday *May 15*	A swarm of flies invades Brighton beach. A major forest fire blazes in the Gwydyr Forest, above the Conway Valley in Snowdonia.
Friday *May 16*	Glen Martin (9), from Harolds Hill, Essex, opens the new Dartford Tunnel under the river Thames at noon. 959km of the Peak National Park are closed because of fire risk.
Saturday *May 17*	Mounted policemen search the M55 motorway for a Monitor Lizard over 1.8m long! The biggest loaf of bread in the world, 4.5m tall and weighing more than 363kg, is cut into 2,000 pieces and sold for charity in Tewkesbury, Glos.
Sunday *May 18*	There is another massive eruption of Mount St Helens in the USA. Tremors can be felt 300km away, the whole area has to be evacuated.
Monday *May 19*	At a meeting in Canberra, Australia, 15 countries sign an agreement to conserve krill and other marine creatures in the Antarctic.
Tuesday *May 20*	Stephen Trafford and his father John break the record for visiting all 268 stations on the London Underground in 18 hours 3mins.
Wednesday *May 21*	A solar flare that lasts 40mins is recorded by Solar Max, which was launched on Feb 14. It's one of the longest ever! The Chelsea Flower Show opens in London.
Thursday *May 22*	Swarms of Belgian brown-tailed moth caterpillars have reached London. It's taken them several years to make their way from the east coast.
Friday *May 23*	The European space rocket *Ariane* makes a flight of 288 seconds and crashes into the sea near Devil's Island off French Guiana.
Saturday *May 24*	Re-enactment of the Rainhill Trials nr Liverpool, when Stephenson's *Rocket* won first prize and was chosen as the best steam engine in 1829.
Sunday *May 25*	Mount St Helens erupts again, sending another huge column of ash into the sky. The crater is now about 4km wide and over 1,500m deep.
Monday *May 26*	Bank Holiday. The 23rd Milk Race, the most famous cycling race in Britain, starts at Southend. The Soviet Union launches two cosmonauts, one of them Hungarian, in a Soyuz-36 spacecraft to link up with the orbiting space lab Salyut-6.

Tuesday *May 27*	Salt water algae called Prymnesium, which kills fresh water fish, has reappeared at Hickling Broad in Norfolk for the first time in 11yrs.
Wednesday *May 28*	NASA reports that their Pioneer Venus I space craft, which has been orbiting the planet Venus since 1978, has found mountains higher than Everest. They will be named after goddesses!
Thursday *May 29*	Oak Apple Day: the anniversary of the Restoration to the throne of King Charles II in 1660. The Army rejects plans for new bottle-green uniforms. Full Moon
Friday *May 30*	Thirty-five of the original 'Little Ships' re-enact the rescue of Allied troops from Dunkirk during World War II in 1940. They take 9hrs to cross the Channel.
Saturday *May 31*	A lock of hair belonging to the composer Franz Schubert is sold in New York for more than £325.

Robert Stephenson's steam engine, the *Rocket*, reached the unheard of speed of 35mph when it won the Rainhill Trials in 1829. It also succeeded in pulling wagons at an average speed of 11mph. Sadly, it also became the first steam engine to be involved in a fatal accident. William Huskisson, the Liverpool Member of Parliament, slipped on the track at the Grand Opening of the Liverpool to Manchester Railway in 1830.

A huge cloud of volcanic dust from Mount St Helens closes roads and stops trains and planes in the north west of the USA.

June

Sunday *June 1*	Sponsored Dog Jog in Regents Park, London, in aid of the Spinal Injuries Association.
Monday *June 2*	Two osprey eggs hatch at Loch Garten, Speyside. 2,000th edition of Granada TV's 'Coronation St'.
Tuesday *June 3*	Two Soviet cosmonauts return to earth in their Soyuz-36 craft after 8 days in space. Dry hot weather continues: 'Use Water Wisely' leaflets are distributed in the West Country.
Wednesday *June 4*	Willie Carson wins the Derby at Epsom for the second year running, this time on *Henbit*, in temperatures of 29°C. An Oliver Cromwell sixpence, dated 1658, is sold in London for £10,000.
Thursday *June 5*	A tornado in Nairn, Scotland, blows over caravans and breaks windows. Celebrations in Crediton, Devon, to mark the 13th centenary of the birth of St Boniface.
Friday *June 6*	A baby puma called Bonny is born at London Zoo. She weighs just under half a kilo.
Saturday *June 7*	The Milk Cup cycling race finishes at Blackpool. Start of the 6th single-handed Transatlantic Yacht Race at Plymouth.
Sunday *June 8*	Work stops on the new Beccles bypass, Suffolk, because of a mute swan's nest with 7 eggs in it. Swans are protected by law and the eggs must be allowed to hatch, which normally takes about 28 days.
Monday *June 9*	Hot weather causes ornamental fish fatalities in Brighton, where 50 carp and several goldfish are found floating belly up in Queen's Park.
Tuesday *June 10*	The clock stops on the Liver Building in Liverpool when thieves steal the mechanism that makes it work. Prince Charles opens a Bottle Bank at Buckingham Palace.
Wednesday *June 11*	A team of experts start a survey of the Great Wall of China to assess the damage caused by people helping themselves to the stone! New Moon
Thursday *June 12*	The search for oil off the Kent and Sussex coasts starts with a survey of the seabed between Folkestone and Eastbourne. Sir Billy Butlin, who started the first holiday camp at Skegness in 1934, dies aged 80.
Friday *June 13*	Mount St Helens in the USA erupts again. A huge mushroom-shaped cloud of ash is blown up into the sky.

June

Takes its name from the great goddess Juno, or from 'juniores', the Latin word for young people, who were honoured this month.
'Zomer-maand' in Old Dutch (summer month) and 'Seremonath' in Old Saxon (dry month).

Osprey (Pandion Haliaetus) disappeared from the British Isles at the beginning of this century. In the mid-1950s the first pair returned and nested near Loch Garten, Speyside, Scotland. Since then, the numbers have gradually increased and the nests and eggs are carefully guarded by the RSPB.

In 1980, 25 pairs of osprey nest in Scotland and 22 of them lay eggs. From these 41 young are fledged. They leave in the autumn and spend the winter in West Africa.

Happy Birthday, Happy Birthday, Your Highness, Your Highness!

The kings and queens of the United Kingdom have had two birthdays each year since the time of William IV (1765–1837). An official birthday was fixed for the middle of summer (the 2nd or 3rd Saturday in June) because that is the best time for outdoor celebrations, parades and processions. Curiously, most recent monarchs have been born in the spring or summer anyway!

Royal Birthdays

William IV	August 21 1765
Victoria	May 24 1819
Edward VII	November 9 1841
George V	June 3 1865
Edward VIII	June 23 1894
George VI	December 14 1895
Elizabeth II	April 21 1926

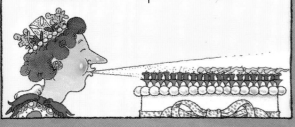

The Universe ●
10,000,000 THREATENED BY FAMINE IN EAST AFRICA

Beaver ▲
WETTEST JUNE IN ENGLAND FOR 101 YEARS

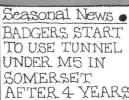

Seasonal News ●
BADGERS START TO USE TUNNEL UNDER M5 IN SOMERSET AFTER 4 YEARS

Yodel ■
US CRUISE MISSILES TO BE BASED AT GREENHAM COMMON

Saturday *June 14*	The Queen's official birthday. Walter Cousins, who has delivered milk to No. 10 Downing St for the last 10 years, is awarded the British Empire Medal in the Birthday Honours.
Sunday *June 15*	Thunderstorms in central and south-east England cause floods, after the driest May and June for 50 years. Nearly 9cm of rain fall in Sussex over the weekend.
Monday *June 16*	Mars, Mercury and Sullivan, the shire horses who deliver beer in the City of London, start their holiday at a hop farm in Kent. Sullivan, who has taken part in the Lord Mayor's show since 1969, retires later this year.
Tuesday *June 17*	Richard Adams, who wrote *Watership Down*, is elected the new president of the RSPCA. A Colorado beetle is identified on Dover beach.
Wednesday *June 18*	The swan's eggs, which have delayed the Beccles bypass since June 8, have hatched. The road will be called 'Swans Way' in their honour!
Thursday *June 19*	The Olympic Flame is kindled from the sun's rays at Olympia in Greece. It will be taken by relay to Moscow for the Games.
Friday *June 20*	4 nurses from University College Hospital in London start a sponsored cycle ride from John O'Groats to Land's End. Summer solstice
Saturday *June 21*	A memorial to the writer George Eliot is unveiled in Poet's Corner, Westminster Abbey. Her real name was Mary Ann Evans.
Sunday *June 22*	Joyce Cansfield, from Otley in Yorkshire, becomes the new National Scrabble Champion: she scores 1540 points in three games.
Monday *June 23*	First day of the Lawn Tennis Championships at Wimbledon. An electronic 'eye' is used for the first time this year to help the linesmen. Beep Beep
Tuesday *June 24*	Midsummer's Day. A new vaccine against bee and wasp stings is launched: it is made out of pure bee and wasp venom. Real Tennis is 450 years old! Torrential rain at Wimbledon.
Wednesday *June 25*	Philip Weld (65) wins the 6th Transatlantic Yacht Race, knocking $2\frac{1}{2}$ days off the previous record.
Thursday *June 26*	A crossing for cows, with traffic lights and warning signs, has been installed at Nether Stowey, Somerset.

Friday *June 27*	A new unmanned lightship costing £350,000 is delivered to Trinity House. It will be anchored near the Channel Isles and has a 30,000 candle-power light with a range of 27km. Full Moon
Saturday *June 28*	A 3.5m python is missing in Gothenburg, Sweden, after it disappeared down a lavatory!
Sunday *June 29*	The Soviet Union launches an unmanned spacecraft to take supplies to the two cosmonauts who have been orbiting earth since April in the Salyut-6 space station.
Monday *June 30*	The sixpence (2½p) is no longer legal tender. Iceland elects its first woman President, Vigdis Finnbogadottir.

Top Tens of The Year 1980

Top Ten Single Artists
(According to the *NME*)

1. Madness
2. Blondie
3. Diana Ross
4. Sheena Easton
5. Abba
6. The Police
7. David Bowie
8. UB40
9. Odyssey
10. The Beat

Top Ten Singles
(According to the *NME*)

1. Crying (Don McLean)
2. Woman In Love (Barbara Streisand)
3. 9 to 5 (Sheena Easton)
4. Funkytown (Lipps Inc.)
5. No Doubt About It (Hot Chocolate)
5. Working My Way Back To You (Detroit Spinners)
7. Theme from MASH (The Mash)
8. Feels Like I'm In Love (Kelly Marie)
8. Upside Down (Diana Ross)
10. Use It Up and Wear It Out (Odyssey)

Top Ten Toys
(According to the British Association of Toy Retailers)

1. Action Man
2. Computer Battleships
3. Connect 4
4. Tool Kit (Fisher Price)
5. Space Lego
6. Skates (Morris Vulcan)
7. Rubik's Cube
8. Cindy's Electronic Cooker
9. Electronic Space Invaders Game
10. Star Wars Figures

Top Ten Films
(According to Screen International)

1. Kramer v. Kramer
2. The Empire Strikes Back
3. Alien
4. The Black Hole
5. 10
6. Monty Python's Life of Brian
7. Star Trek—The Motion Picture
8. Airplane
9. Escape from Alcatraz
10. The Aristocats

July

Tuesday *July 1*	Canada gets a new national anthem, 'O Canada'. British athletes Sebastian Coe and Steve Ovett set new world records in Oslo: Coe runs 1000m in 2min 13.4secs and Ovett covers the mile in 3mins 48.8secs.
Wednesday *July 2*	The RSPB reserve at Minsmere, Suffolk, wins the Council for Europe's diploma for conservation work. The EEC has agreed to ban the import of all whale products.
Thursday *July 3*	Dame Naomi James breaks the women's record for crossing the Atlantic. She arrives at Newport, Rhode Island, USA, at 9.11am BST, having completed the voyage in 25 days 19 hours.
Friday *July 4*	Evonne Cawley, from Australia, wins the Women's Singles title at Wimbledon for the second time.
Saturday *July 5*	Bjorn Borg, from Sweden, wins the Men's Singles title at Wimbledon for the 5th year running. He beats John McEnroe in 5 sets.
Sunday *July 6*	A plaque to Frank Richards, who created Billy Bunter, is unveiled at his home in Percy Ave, Broadstairs, Kent.
Monday *July 7*	From today, breakfast (fruit juice, cornflakes, egg, bacon and sausage) on British Rail's InterCity trains costs £5.
Tuesday *July 8*	The Church of England put up their charges: a baptism certificate will go up by 15p to 75p, a wedding by £5 to £25 and a funeral service by £4 to £20.
	Earth tremors at Stoke-on-Trent
Wednesday *July 9*	The Post Office issues four new stamps showing famous authoresses. Earthquakes in Greece measure 6.3, 5.9 and 5.4 on the Richter Scale.
Thursday *July 10*	Alexandra Palace in north London is badly damaged by fire. Gerard d'Aboville sets out from Cape Cod, Mass, USA to row across the Atlantic in his black and yellow boat *Captain Cook*.
Friday *July 11*	Prince Charles opens the new Britannia Bridge across the Menai Strait to Anglesey. *HMS Invincible* (19,500 tonnes), the largest warship built in Britain since World War II, is commissioned at Portsmouth. New Moon
Saturday *July 12*	*Eresus Niger*, a rare breed of spider which looks rather like a ladybird and was thought to be extinct, has been found in heathland in Dorset.

July

Named in honour of Julius Caesar. The Old Dutch name was 'Hooy-maand' (hay month) and the Old Saxon name was 'Maedd-monath' because the cattle were turned into the meadow to feed.

The XXII Olympic Games in Moscow

Only 5784 competitors from 81 nations take part in the Moscow Olympics because some countries are boycotting the Games in protest at the Soviet invasion of Afghanistan. Altogether 54 countries are missing, which makes quite a difference to the medals tables.

The USSR wins 195 medals (80 gold), East Germany wins 126 medals (47 gold) and Bulgaria wins 40 (8 gold). Britain wins 21 medals altogether (5 gold, 7 silver and 9 bronze).

Britain's Gold Medals

Athletics: 1500m (Sebastian Coe)
800m (Steve Ovett)
Decathlon (Daley Thompson)
100m (Allan Wells)
Swimming: 100m Breaststroke
(Duncan Goodhew)

Allan Wells of Scotland, becomes only the second Briton ever (the first was Harold Abrahams in 1924) to win the men's 100m sprint.

The Olympic Flame is carried by runners more than 4800km through four different countries from Greece to Moscow. It is brought into the Lenin Stadium for the opening ceremony by the Soviet basketball captain, Serge Belov.

After the opening parades, a special message from outer space flashes onto the giant computer screens. The two Soviet cosmonauts orbiting Earth in the Salyut-6 space station wish the competitors 'courage, good luck and spectacular victories'.

COURAGE, GOOD LUCK, SPECTAC-ULAR VICTORIES

July 9: Famous Women Writers

12P Charlotte Brontë: Jane Eyre
13½P George Eliot: The Mill on the Floss
15P Emily Brontë: Wuthering Heights
17½P Mrs Gaskell: North and South

Sunday July 13	Hundreds of people collapse at the Holinwell Show near Kirkby in Ashfield, Nottinghamshire, during a children's marching band contest.
Monday July 14	Beginning of Ramadan. The United Nations 'Decade for Women' conference opens in Copenhagen. It is the mid-point of the decade launched during International Women's Year in 1975.
Tuesday July 15	St Swithin's Day. First birthday of an electric motor, invented by a clockmaker in Kidderminster. In one year, at 120rpm, the motor has turned round 63,722,800 times—fuelled by the juice of one lemon!
Wednesday July 16	The early warning aircraft Nimrod makes its maiden flight.
Thursday July 17	The Humber Bridge is finished! It's the longest single-span suspension bridge in the world. The overall length is 2220m and the main span 1410m.
Friday July 18	The Olympic Flame arrives in Moscow. India puts a 35.8kg satellite *Rohina* into orbit.
Saturday July 19	President Brezhnev opens the XXII Olympic Games at Moscow's Lenin Stadium. Teams from 81 different countries compete.
Sunday July 20	His Divine Holiness Shree Pramukh Swami, the spiritual leader of millions of Hindus, rides 8km on an elephant from Alperton High School to Meadow Garth in Neasden, London, to consecrate the site for the largest Hindu temple outside India.
Monday July 21	Eric Tabarly leaves Sandy Hook, New Jersey, USA, to sail across the Atlantic in his trimaran *Paul Ricard*.
Tuesday July 22	Duncan Goodhew wins Britain's first gold medal at the Moscow Olympics—the 100m breaststroke.
Wednesday July 23	Lt Col Pham Tuan, the first Vietnamese spaceman, and Col Viktor Gorbatko are launched in a Soyuz spacecraft to link up with the orbiting space lab Salyut-6.
Thursday July 24	The two baby osprey, who hatched at Loch Garten, Speyside, on June 2, fly for the first time. Peter Sellers dies.
Friday July 25	Allan Wells, from Edinburgh, wins the 100m gold medal at the Moscow Olympics with a time of 10.25 seconds.

Saturday *July 26*	Daley Thompson wins a gold medal at the Moscow Olympics in the decathlon. He scores a total of 8495 points.
Sunday *July 27*	Paul Caffey, from New Zealand, and Nigel Dennis, from Anglesey, who set off from Holyhead on May 5, arrive back after paddling 3520km in kayaks round the coast of Britain. Full Moon
Monday *July 28*	New rules for ice-cream vans: chimes can only be sounded when the van is moving and in 4 second bursts. They should not exceed 800 decibels at a distance of 182.8m!
Tuesday *July 29*	A pair of 4-year-old brown kiwis are presented to London Zoo by Auckland Zoological Park, New Zealand.
Wednesday *July 30*	A 2,000,000-year-old fossilized starfish, which was dug up on Canvey Island, is presented to the Riverside Museum.
Thursday *July 31*	25°C in Reykjavik, the capital of Iceland—the hottest day in living memory there! Princess Alice, Duchess of Gloucester, unveils a statue of Richard III in Leicester.

Champions of 1980

Puppy of the Year	Halfmoon of Olac (West Highland terrier)
Supreme Champion at Crufts	Shargleam Blackcap (retriever)
Supreme Champion at Smithfield	Panda of Westdrums (579kg)
Conker Champion	Keith Height (23) from Brigstock
Junior Cook of the Year	Michelle Wood (14) from Liverpool
Newsboy/Newsgirl of the Year	Heather Turner (16) from Derbyshire
Milkman of the Year	Dennis Buckley from Abbey Wood
Young Musician of the Year	Nicholas Daniel (18) from Winchester
Musician of the Year	Jacqueline du Pré
Crossword Puzzle Champion	Dr John Sykes
Mastermind	Fred Housego
BBC TV Personality of the Year	Penelope Keith
ITV TV Personality of the Year	Benny Hill
Museum of the Year	Natural History Museum, London
Motor racing World Champion	Alan Jones (Australia)
American Academy of Motion Picture Arts and Science's	
Best Film	Kramer v. Kramer
Best Actress	Sally Field
Best Actor	Dustin Hoffman

August

Friday *August 1*	Eric Tabarly in his trimaran *Paul Ricard*, arrives at the Lizard in Cornwall after sailing across the Atlantic. He breaks the record by nearly 2 days. Sebastian Coe wins the 1500m gold medal at the Moscow Olympics in 3 min 38.4 secs.
Saturday *August 2*	Frederica, the oldest goldfish in Britain, dies, aged 40, in her pond at Worthing, Sussex.
Sunday *August 3*	Closing ceremony at the Olympic Games in Moscow. Britain won 5 gold, 7 silver and 9 bronze medals.
Monday *August 4*	Happy 80th birthday to Queen Elizabeth, the Queen Mother! She gets 20 sacks of cards and letters, 30 birthday cakes and 1400 telegrams, not to mention a string of bonfires along the Kent/Sussex coast and a special new stamp in her honour!
Tuesday *August 5*	Prince Charles dives down to the *Mary Rose*, which sank off Portsmouth in 1545.
Wednesday *August 6*	One minute's silence at 8.15am in Hiroshima, Japan, to mark the exact time that the first atomic bomb was dropped there 35yrs ago.
Thursday *August 7*	Hurricane Allen, which has devastated the islands of St Lucia, Jamaica, Cuba and Haiti in the Caribbean, rushes on towards the Gulf of Mexico at 280kph.
Friday *August 8*	40th anniversary of the Battle of Britain in World War II.
Saturday *August 9*	The UK Viking I spacecraft runs out of steering gas after 4 years on its 1489th orbit of Mars.
Sunday *August 10*	9th annual Birdman Event at Bognor Regis, Sussex. More than 40 competitors try to fly 50m off the end of the pier. New Moon
Monday *August 11*	Mike Read, from Sproughton, nr Ipswich, becomes the first person to swim the English Channel backwards. It takes him 14hrs 52mins and lots of jellyfish stings.
Tuesday *August 12*	Ching Ching, the Giant Panda, returns to London Zoo after 5 months in hospital. She has had a special micro-chip radio transmitter fitted to warn of any recurrence of her illness.
Wednesday *August 13*	The 20 millionth person visits the Cheddar Gorge Caves today. They first opened in 1927.

Thursday *August 14*	Earth tremor in Burslem, Staffordshire. Mavis Hutchinson (55) arrives at Land's End after running more than 1344km from John O'Groats in 16 days 21hrs 55mins.
Friday *August 15*	Gerry Breen (27) wins Britain's first hang-glider race, from Land's End to John O'Groats, in 4 days.
Saturday *August 16*	French fishermen blockade Channel ports: about 15,000 British holidaymakers are stuck on the Continent.
Sunday *August 17*	The 1446.9m Hekla volcano erupts in southern Iceland.

Earth tremor in Kidsgrove, Staffordshire

August

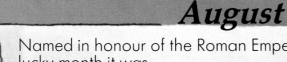

Named in honour of the Roman Emperor Augustus, whose lucky month it was.
The Old Dutch name was 'Oost-maand'—harvest month.
The Old Saxon name was 'Weod-monath'—weed month.

Mount Everest was first climbed in 1953 by Edmund Hillary, from New Zealand, and the Sherpa, Tenzing Norgay. Since then, another 85 mountaineers have climbed it. Reinhold Messner is the first to reach the summit on his own and without oxygen. The first solo climb ever (with oxygen) was made in 1978 by Franz Oppurg, from Austria. The first Britons to reach the summit were Douglas Scott and Dougal Haston in 1975. Three women have reached the summit of Everest—the first was Junko Tabei, from Japan, in 1975.

The Queen Mother's 80th birthday stamp

ELIZABETH
HER MAJESTY QUEEN
THE QUEEN MOTHER
12P
80TH BIRTHDAY

Hurricanes have a minimum speed of 120kph and they whirl in an anti-clockwise direction in the northern hemisphere, and in a clockwise direction in the southern hemisphere. Their name comes from a Caribbean word meaning 'the spirit of evil'. Up until 1975, hurricanes were always given female names. Then the Australians decided this was totally unfair, and ever since male names have alternated with female names.

Monday August 18	Reinhold Messner, an Italian mountaineer, sets out alone from his base camp to climb Mount Everest (8847.7m) along the north ridge route from Tibet.
Tuesday August 19	A 2-tonne bronze cannon, embossed with the Tudor Rose, is raised from the wreck of the *Mary Rose* in the Solent.
Wednesday August 20	Reinhold Messner becomes the first man ever to climb Mount Everest (8847.7m) on his own and without oxygen.
Thursday August 21	There is the biggest swarm of shooting stars at Chichester in Sussex since 1946!
Friday August 22	A cloud of yellow dust (called a 'calima') from the Sahara desert blots out the sun in central Spain and causes a heatwave.
Saturday August 23	A grizzly bear called Hercules vanishes on the island of Benbecula in the Hebrides. He was taking part in a film but swam out to sea.
Sunday August 24	Voyager 1, which has now passed Jupiter, speeds on towards Saturn at 73,040kph.
Monday August 25	Bank Holiday. National Parascending Championships at Grantham, Lincs. Andy Cowley makes 3 perfect landings on a 10cm disc.
Tuesday August 26	The National Aboriginal Conference protests against drilling for oil at Noonkanbah in NW Australia. It's the home of the Great Goanna (Lizard) spirit. Full Moon
Wednesday August 27	Steve Ovett sets a new 1500m world record of 3mins 31.4secs in Coblenz, East Germany.
Thursday August 28	A new French apple called 'Ozark Gold' is born: it will be ready for picking about 10 days before the British 'Discovery'.
Friday August 29	Margaret Hicks (47), reaches Southampton in her sloop *Anonymous Bay* and is the first woman to complete a two-way crossing of the Atlantic in a monohull.
Saturday August 30	32 Chieftain tanks prepare to leave Tidworth in Hampshire at the beginning of Army exercise 'Crusader 80'.
Sunday August 31	A 6-man team of 4 soldiers and 2 marines cross the English Channel by parachute. They jump from their aircraft above Dover Castle and land nr Sangatte in France 22 mins later.

September

Monday *September 1*	The sun's rays set off the fire alarm in Canterbury Cathedral and 4 fire engines rush to the rescue.
Tuesday *September 2*	Mount Etna in Sicily erupts: lava streams down and rocks are hurled in the air. Geoff Boycott scores a century in the Centenary Test at Lords.
Wednesday *September 3*	The Post Office has given special permission for Sponne School at Towcester, Northants, to bring out a stamp to celebrate its 550th anniversary.
Thursday *September 4*	Big Ben (the Great Clock of the Palace of Westminster) gets his 4 faces cleaned this week—for the first time in 3 years.
Friday *September 5*	Gerard d'Aboville spends his 35th birthday rowing across the Atlantic (see July 10). The world's longest road tunnel, underneath the St Gotthard mountains in Switzerland, is opened.
Saturday *September 6*	Scientists identify another moon orbiting Jupiter from photographs sent back from Voyager 1. It brings the total number of Jupiter's moons to 16.
Sunday *September 7*	8 firemen from Eastbourne in Sussex set out to swim 240km of the river Thames from Lechlade to Westminster in relays—underwater!
Monday *September 8*	A reading survey carried out by the Assistant Masters and Mistresses Association says that *Beano*, *Dandy* and *Nutty* are the most popular comics.
Tuesday *September 9*	A world ploughing marathon record of 149hrs 37mins is claimed by John Shave of East Harling in Norfolk. New Moon
Wednesday *September 10*	The Post Office issues four new stamps showing famous British conductors.
Thursday *September 11*	Jewish New Year AM 5741. A new Wildlife and Countryside Bill bans adult (over 10 months) bulls from being on their own in fields crossed by footpaths. They are allowed if accompanied by cows or heifers.
Friday *September 12*	Force 10 gales and torrential rain in the north of England and Scotland. A gust of 130.8kph is recorded in Edinburgh.
Saturday *September 13*	10,000 balloons are released at the start of Thamesday in London. Hercules, the grizzly bear who vanished in the Hebrides 3 weeks ago, is found safe and well.

Sunday *September 14*	Dr John Sykes, editor of the Concise and the Pocket Oxford Dictionaries, wins *The Times* National Crossword Puzzle Championship. He does 4 puzzles in 37.5mins!
Monday *September 15*	The Grand Opera House in Belfast reopens tonight 8 years after it was closed by a bomb. Prince Charles is presented with an international diving licence. He has made 5 dives down to the wreck of the *Mary Rose* in the Solent.
Tuesday *September 16*	Sealink's last passenger-only steamship, the 3992 tonne *Caesarea*, will make its final Channel crossing at the end of the month.
Wednesday *September 17*	Westminster City Council decide to save the Christmas Tree in Trafalgar Square, London, despite spending cuts. The tree is a present from the people of Oslo, but it costs £5,000 to transport it from the docks, put it up and illuminate it.
Thursday *September 18*	The skeleton of a horse, dating from the 10th century, is found in a cesspit in Ironmonger Lane in the City of London.
Friday *September 19*	Southend Pier, due to close at the end of the month, has been saved by local protest and the Poet Laureate, Sir John Betjeman.
Saturday *September 20*	Yom Kippur, the Jewish Day of Atonement, the holiest day of the Jewish year. Gerard d'Aboville arrives at Ushant after rowing alone across the Atlantic in 71 days 23 hours.
Sunday *September 21*	The new Peace Pagoda at Milton Keynes, Buckinghamshire, is inaugurated. An elephant leads a procession of monks from 7 different countries.
Monday *September 22*	'Chitty Chitty Bang Bang' is sold at the British Car Auctions at Farnborough, Hampshire, for £15,000.
Tuesday *September 23*	A larger-than-life head of the god Mercury, carved in about AD 150 out of yellow Cotswold limestone, and found at Uley, Glos., goes on show at the British Museum in London.
Wednesday *September 24*	The Good Toy Guide is launched by the Toy Libraries Association. Richard Noble sets a British land speed record of 248.87mph over one mile in his jet car *Thrust 2* at RAF Greenham Common, Berks. Full Moon
Thursday *September 25*	Richard Noble sets another British land speed record at RAF Greenham Common: he reaches 251.19mph over one kilometre in *Thrust 2*.

Friday *September 26*	Bristol University launches an appeal to save rare wild plants at the Lizard, Cornwall. They are threatened by the Rambling Hottentot Fig, which was introduced in 1881: it smothers smaller plants.
Saturday *September 27*	The Queen opens her orchards at Sandringham in Norfolk so that people can pick her Cox's Orange Pippins.
Sunday *September 28*	18,000 runners take part in the 3rd *Sunday Times* Fun Run in Hyde Park in London.
Monday *September 29*	Col Ronald Gardner-Thorpe is elected the 653rd Lord Mayor of London.
Tuesday *September 30*	A 4-month-old pony called Raven's Revel falls into a swimming pool at Roundhill, Tipton St John, Devon. Firemen have to drain the pool to get him out.

September

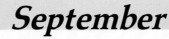

This was the seventh month when the year used to start in March.
The Old Dutch name was 'Herst-maand'—autumn month.
The Old Saxon name was 'Gerst-monath'—barley month.

The iron pier at Southend-on-Sea was built in 1889, complete with Pavilion and the first electric railway of its kind in England. It replaced an old wooden pier where horse-drawn trams used to trot up and down. Stretching 2.8km into the sea, it's the longest pleasure pier in the world.

September 10:
Four new
stamps
honouring
British
conductors

October

Wednesday *October 1*	The two Soviet cosmonauts, Leonid Popov and Valery Ryumin, who have been in the orbiting space station Salyut-6 since April, break the space endurance record of 175 days 36 mins. Friends of the Earth is 10 years old today.
Thursday *October 2*	Charlie Brown is 30. The final section of the M90 from the Forth Bridge to Perth is opened today.
Friday *October 3*	The Advanced Passenger Train demonstrates its paces for the Press. It whizzes round the curve at Bushey, Hertfordshire at 200kph and the one at Leighton Buzzard at 176kph.
Saturday *October 4*	The wreck of a warship, found in the Solent near Portsmouth, has been named as the first *HMS Invincible*, which sank in 1758.
Sunday *October 5*	The Cory Band from South Wales wins the 1980 European Brass Band Championships at the Albert Hall in London.
Monday *October 6*	Scotland's first long-distance footpath, the West Highland Way, is opened. It runs from Milngavie, north of Glasgow, to Fort William.
Tuesday *October 7*	Torrential rain and winds up to 137.6kph in the West Country. 3.8cm rain falls in 12 hours on Dartmoor and Bodmin Moor. There is a heavy hail storm in south London.
Wednesday *October 8*	The Austin Metro, the long-awaited successor to the Mini, is launched today.
Thursday *October 9*	Jaromir Wagner flies across the Atlantic from Frankfurt to New York strapped to the top of a twin-engined Islander aircraft. He wears long johns, a wet suit, two leather motor cycle suits, three pairs of socks and a crash helmet. New Moon
Friday *October 10*	Hang gliding has been banned in East Germany.
Saturday *October 11*	Soviet cosmonauts Leonid Popov and Valery Ryumin land in Central Asia after spending 185 days on board Salyut-6. They have grown 7.6cm while they've been in space!
Sunday *October 12*	16th World Conker Championship at Ashton, nr Oundle, Northants. Keith Height (23) from Brigstock is the youngest ever winner.
Monday *October 13*	Margaret Thatcher was born in 1925. Eight Queen Bees are stolen during a raid on the Buckfast Abbey beehives on Dartmoor.

October

This was the eighth month in the old Roman calendar when the year started in March.
The Old Dutch name was 'Wyn-maand'—wine month.
The Old English name was 'Winter-fylleth'—winter full moon.

Space Ace!

Flight Engineer Valery Ryumin spent 175 days on board the orbiting space station Salyut-6 in 1979, a new space endurance record.

   This year, he and Commander Leonid Popov set a new space endurance record of 185 days on board Salyut-6. Altogether, Ryumin has spent very nearly a year of his life in outer space. While in orbit, the cosmonauts spend their time carrying out experiments, doing repairs and looking after the miniature garden. When they get back to Earth, they are made Heroes of the Soviet Union.

Rhinos in Danger!

Rhinos have been hunted for centuries—especially for their horn, which is believed to have all sorts of magic powers, as well as being used as a medicine. The African Black or Hook-Lipped Rhinoceros (*Diceros bicornis*) has two horns, with the large front one measuring about 60cm. 50 years ago much larger ones were found—the record being 136cm. The African White or Square-Lipped Rhinoceros (*Diceros simus*) also has two horns with the front one measuring between 90–140cm. The record is 157.5cm. The Indian Rhinoceros (*Rhinoceros unicornis*) has only one horn, which grows to about 60cm.

Buckfast Bees

The Buckfast Bee was bred by Brother Adam, a Benedictine monk, who is now 82 years old. It is noted for its good health and good temper. There are ten Buckfast apiaries, with 320 hives that produce honey, and another 130 hives for breeding Buckfast Queens.

The Beacon
PAIR OF NAPOLEON'S BLACK SILK SOCKS SOLD FOR £50 IN MONTE CARLO

Neptune
LAMB WAR WITH FRANCE ENDS

Daily Migration
2.9 KG ONION, 31.3 KG MARROW AND 103.9 KG PUMPKIN TAKE PART IN GIANT VEG CONTEST IN LONDON

Scroll
HUGE ANTI-NUCLEAR DEMO: 50,000 MARCH THROUGH LONDON

Tuesday *October 14*	The World Wildlife Fund starts a campaign to save the wild rhino. A new UN Treaty proposes that the moon becomes 'a common heritage' and 'shall not become the property of any state, international, inter-governmental or non-governmental organization'.
Wednesday *October 15*	*The Old Man of Lochnagar* by Prince Charles is published today. He wrote it 11 years ago for his younger brothers Andrew and Edward.
Thursday *October 16*	Heavy rain in London and the south east: the London Underground is flooded. A new oil well is found in the North Sea, about 192km NE of Aberdeen.
Friday *October 17*	The Voyager spacecraft approaches Saturn. Mount St Helens in the USA erupts again.
Saturday *October 18*	The 5280km Himalayan Car Rally starts in Bombay. The Thurrock Marching Brass from Essex wins the British Marching Bands Championship at Wembley.
Sunday *October 19*	Leuchars, Fife, has its earliest snow for 50 years. Survey ships check the exact location of the Goodwin Sands, off Ramsgate, after the Walmer lifeboat ran aground twice last week.
Monday *October 20*	For sale in Folkestone: a Martello Tower, built in 1805, when Napoleon threatened to invade Britain. It's still got its cannonball stores!
Tuesday *October 21*	The red kite has had its most successful breeding season this century: 21 pairs have reared 27 young in central Wales.
Wednesday *October 22*	Cocky, a sulphur-crested cockatoo from London Zoo, is presented with a long-service medal by the Burlington Arcade Association for entertaining visitors for over 50 years.
Thursday *October 23*	Police warn motorists to watch out for swans standing on the M5 motorway, mistaking it for a river. Full Moon
Friday *October 24*	United Nations Day. A severe earthquake in southern Mexico measures between 6 and 6.5 on the Richter Scale and lasts for 3mins 17secs.
Saturday *October 25*	FOR SALE: the Rose and Crown in Hempstead, nr Saffron Walden, Essex, the public house where Dick Turpin was born in 1705.
Sunday *October 26*	Ernest Conner runs the New York Marathon backwards. End of the Himalayan Car Rally—only half of the 75 starters finish.

Monday *October 27*	The Queen is greeted in Morocco with milk and dates—the traditional welcome for important guests. A 50-year-old adult gorilla skeleton is sold for £800 at Christie's in London.
Tuesday *October 28*	Japan and Russia sign agreements not to catch more than 3120 Minke whales each this year. Voyager 1 has discovered 2 new moons orbiting Saturn.
Wednesday *October 29*	The 'Churkey' is launched in London: it's a tiny turkey that tastes like a chicken!
Thursday *October 30*	The Night Ferry train from Victoria Station, London, sets off on its last journey to Gare du Nord in Paris.
Friday *October 31*	Hallowe'en. The *London Evening News* publishes its last edition.

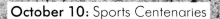

October 10: Sports Centenaries

A Cold Wet Summer with Spectacular Sunsets

The eruptions at Mount St Helens in Washington State, USA, earlier this year, blew the summit off the 2949m mountain and reduced its height to 2528m. They also opened a crater more than 1.6km long and 500m deep.

The giant blasts sent plumes of volcanic ash and steam 18,000m into the sky, and set off huge forest fires, mudslides and floods. The water temperature of the river Toutle rose to 40°C, killing all the fish. Molten rocks swept down the mountain and flattened every tree within a 310 sq km area.

The eruption on May 18 was equal to approximately 100 million tonnes of TNT, about 500 times as powerful as the atomic bomb dropped on Hiroshima.

Some weather experts think that the huge concentration of dust in the stratosphere from Mount St Helens changed the weather this year. They blame the cold wet summer on the volcano but also say that it produced some spectacular sunsets!

November

Saturday November 1

Lancelot, the Bewick's Swan, with his mate Elaine, and their 2 cygnets, arrives back from the Arctic. It's his 18th winter at the Wildfowl Trust at Slimbridge, Glos.

Sunday November 2

RAC London to Brighton Veteran Car Rally. 282 cars (all built before Dec 31, 1904) take part. The winner is an 1899 Rochest Tricycle which takes 2hrs 20mins.

Monday November 3

Voyager 1 approaches Saturn's largest moon, Titan. With a diameter of 5760km, it is the biggest moon in the universe!

Tuesday November 4

Presidential election in USA: Ronald Reagan (69) wins and becomes the oldest President ever. BBC announces that Peter Davison (29) is to be the 5th and youngest Dr Who since the series began in 1963.

Wednesday November 5

A cold, wet Bonfire Night! Buckingham Palace announces that Princess Anne is expecting her second child in May: the new baby will be 6th in line to the throne.

Thursday November 6

Pictures from *Voyager 1* shows that Saturn is really pale lemon yellow and not white, as previously thought.

Friday November 7

Snow causes chaos in southern England and Wales. Icy winds blow in from Russia.   New Moon

Saturday November 8

The Lord Mayor's Show in London: the procession is led by Pearly Kings and Queens and Chelsea Pensioners.

Sunday November 9

Remembrance Sunday. Moslem New Year (AH 1401). Earth tremors at Kidsgrove, Staffs. *Voyager 1* discovers a new moon orbiting round Saturn—the 15th!

Monday November 10

Missing in Winsford, Cheshire: a boa constrictor called Hissing Sid.

Tuesday November 11

The Greenpeace trawler *Rainbow Warrior* sails into St Helier harbour in Jersey after escaping from Spain, where she was under arrest for harassing the whaling fleet.

Wednesday November 12

Voyager 1 gets within 123,200km of Saturn today—the closest yet—and sends back spectacular pictures of the brightly coloured rings.

Thursday November 13

Halfmoon of Olac (known as Emma), a West Highland white terrier from Bury, Lancs, becomes Puppy of the Year at the Dog World Show in London.

November

This was the ninth month in the old Roman calendar when the year started in March.
The old Saxon name was 'Wind-monath'—wind month!
The Old Dutch name was 'Slaght-maand'—slaughter month!

Voyager

The one-tonne Voyager 1 spacecraft was launched from Cape Canaveral on September 5, 1977.

Voyager 1 sends back images of Saturn by radio signals. They take over an hour to cover the 1,520,000,000 kilometres (950,000,000 miles) to Earth. The pictures show that the planet has at least 100 rings round it, and they are much more complicated than previously thought. They look a bit like the grooves in a gramophone record with boulders over 90cm wide in some rings and tiny, tightly packed particles in others. The outer ring seems to be made up of separate threads of rock and ice particles plaited together.

Voyager also sends back some spectacular pictures of Saturn's 15 icy moons.

Daily Fish.
GERMAN COASTER WRECKED ON LUNDY ISLAND

Daily Planet
ROSALIND NOTT BREAKS WOMEN'S WORLD WATER SPEED RECORD, AVERAGING 109.40 MPH

Daily Knib
SACRED SPRING AT BATH FILLED IN

Daily Blah.
SEAL SETS RECORD BY GIVING BIRTH TO PUP OVER 96 K.M. INLAND ON BANKS OF RIVER TRENT

10P

15P

November 19: PO issue the new Christmas stamps

12P

13½P

17½P

Friday *November 14*	Diwali, the Hindu Festival of Lights. A badger gets his head stuck in a wrought iron gate at Bincleaves nr Weymouth and has to be rescued by firemen!
Saturday *November 15*	Start of National Tree Week. The Woodland Trust will plant an oak, ash or beech tree for you for £1.
Sunday *November 16*	International Women's Marathon in Tokyo: Joyce Smith (43) from Watford, wins in 2hrs 30mins 27secs.
Monday *November 17*	President Sadat of Egypt opens the first tunnel under the Suez Canal.
Tuesday *November 18*	Judith Chisholm takes off in her single engine Cessna Centurion in an attempt to beat the record for a solo flight to Australia.
Wednesday *November 19*	The Post Office issues its new Christmas stamps. No singing on trains in Italy from today: the fine is 90,000 lire (£41).
Thursday *November 20*	5 houses, 9 barges, 8 tugboats, 2 oil rigs and a mobile home are lost in Louisiana, USA, when Lake Peigneur is swallowed up in a giant whirlpool when an old salt mine collapses.
Friday *November 21*	One of the most famous diamonds in the world, the 41.28 carat Polar Star, which once belonged to Napoleon's brother, Joseph Bonaparte, is sold for £1,960,828. Full Moon
Saturday *November 22*	Judith Chisholm lands at Port Hedland, Western Australia, and sets a record for the solo flight from England in a single engine aircraft. She took 83 hours!
Sunday *November 23*	Severe earthquakes in Italy measure 6.5 and 4.9 on the Richter Scale: the tremors can be felt as far north as the Austrian border and as far south as Sicily.
Monday *November 24*	Child Benefit goes up today from £4 to £4.75 per week.
Tuesday *November 25*	A mystery beast that might be a puma is terrorising sheep near Llandiloes, Powys: plaster casts of the paw and claw marks are taken to try to identify it!
Wednesday *November 26*	The largest transformer in Britain (731.5m long, 5.5m wide and 5.6m high) leaves Stafford by road to travel to Manchester. The machine weighs 433 tonnes and will take 5 days to travel the 80km.

Thursday November 27	The United Animal Nations opens its first general assembly in Geneva. It will elect a security council and an international court of animal rights. 3 Soviet cosmonauts are launched in a Soyuz T-3 space craft to join Salyut-6.
Friday November 28	5th Annual Circus World Championships in London. Snow and blizzards in the north of England, Scotland and Ulster. 128kph gale force winds on the Northumberland coast.
Saturday November 29	England and Wales defeat Ireland and Scotland 37–33 at Cardiff Arms Park to mark the centenary of the Welsh Rugby Union.
Sunday November 30	18 giant chimneys are demolished in 30 seconds at the disused brickworks at Kempston Hardwick, Beds. The tallest, 'Big Bertha', is nearly 60m tall and made up of 149,649 bricks!

The Things We Did In 1980

Television 1980

10% of British households have 2 or more TVs.

In winter everybody over 5 years old watches, on average, 20 hours of television a week. There are three channels: BBC 1, BBC 2, ITV.

TV licences cost—black and white £12; colour £34. In May, 1980, there were 13,000,000 colour licences and 5,300,000 black and white ones.

Books 1980

More than 48,000 books are published in 1980.
There are over 36,000 new titles and nearly 11,000 reprints and new editions.

Pets 1980

About half the households in Britain have a pet. There are more than 5,000,000 dogs and nearly 5,000,000 cats.

Cinema 1980

There are 1600 cinema screens in Britain. The average weekly cinema audience is just under 2,500,000.

December

Monday *December 1*	The cost of National Health prescriptions goes up to £1.
Tuesday *December 2*	The Jubilee Sailing Trust announces plans to build a £2,000,000 square-rigged ship, which could be sailed by a mixed crew of physically handicapped and able-bodied people. It will be called *Jubilee* and launched in 1982—Maritime England Year.
Wednesday *December 3*	A record £9000 is paid at Earl's Court for the Supreme Champion of the Royal Smithfield Show—*Panda of Westdrums*.
Thursday *December 4*	The Soviet cosmonauts carry out repairs to Salyut-6 on their seventh day on board.
Friday *December 5*	A submarine is dragged backwards for 5km after being caught in the nets of a French trawler in the St George's Channel.
Saturday *December 6*	National Cat Club Championships at Olympia. A new communications satellite is launched from Cape Canaveral in Florida.
Sunday *December 7*	Ice and snow in Scotland and the east of England. The A93 from Perth to Braemar is blocked. More than 15cms of snow in Cleveland and Humberside. New Moon
Monday *December 8*	John Lennon is shot in New York. The world's heaviest turkey, (35.7kg) is sold for £2200 at the British Turkey Federation's contest.
Tuesday *December 9*	Prince Charles starts trekking through the foothills of the Himalayas accompanied by 90 porters and 21 Sherpas.
Wednesday *December 10*	The three Soviet cosmonauts return safely to Earth after spending 2 weeks on board Salyut-6.
Thursday *December 11*	The Christmas tree in Trafalgar Square is lit up by the Mayor of Oslo at 6pm.
Friday *December 12*	One of the world's longest road tunnels, almost 8km long, is opened just south of Lake Lucerne in Switzerland.
Saturday *December 13*	The 150 tonne brigantine *Eye of the Wind* comes home after sailing round the world in Operation Drake.
Sunday *December 14*	Plymouth's Christmas tree, which is nearly 20m tall, is blown over by winds sweeping in from the Atlantic.

Monday *December 15*	The first water begins to flow into the new Kielder reservoir in Northumberland. It will be 12km long and 800m wide and probably won't be completely filled up before 1982!
Tuesday *December 16*	Col Harland Sanders, who invented Kentucky Fried Chicken, dies in Louisville, aged 90. The Nature Protection Agency announces that French frogs are to become a protected species.
Wednesday *December 17*	Ivy, a Kudu African antelope, is born at London Zoo. 10 'Children of Courage' meet Mrs Thatcher at Westminster Abbey.
Thursday *December 18*	The Duke of Edinburgh presents the Commonwealth Expedition 1980 Green Pennant Awards at the Commonwealth Institute.

December

This used to be the tenth month in the old Roman calendar when the year started in March.

Christmas trees cost about £1.30 per 30.5cm this year. BS4075, which was introduced in 1966 and set standards for the perfect British Christmas tree, has been abolished, so they can now be any shape and size. According to BS4075, Christmas trees shouldn't be cut before November, the width of the tree should not be less than 50% or more than 90% of its height, and the needles shouldn't drop before Twelfth Night. Also, the branches should not be more than 22.9cm apart!
PS The traditional Christmas tree is a Norway Spruce. The one in Trafalgar Square this year is 21.3m tall.

Daily Crescendo

TV-AM WINS BREAKFAST FRANCHISE

STONE AGE ART DISCOVERED IN WYE VALLEY

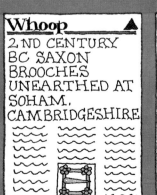

Whoop

2ND CENTURY BC SAXON BROOCHES UNEARTHED AT SOHAM, CAMBRIDGESHIRE

Daily Hedgehog

BAN ON DUTCH CHRYSANTHEMUMS BECAUSE OF WHITE RUST DISEASE

NO PUBLIC TRANSPORT IN LONDON ON CHRISTMAS DAY

Blabber Mouth

LEONARDO DA VINCI'S MANUSCRIPT CODEX LEICESTER SOLD FOR £2.2 MILLION

Friday *December 19*	A plaque to Charlie Chaplin is unveiled at 287 Kennington Road, Lambeth, near where he was born.
Saturday *December 20*	Iris Thomas is ordained as a deacon in the Church of Wales at Llandaff Cathedral. Fine for sleeping in Islington Libraries £50.
Sunday *December 21*	Fred Housego, a London taxi driver, who left school with one GCE 'O' level pass, wins the BBC's 'Mastermind' title. Full Moon
Monday *December 22*	Dozens of cars are glued to a 3km stretch of motorway between Milan and Venice after a very sticky chemical leaks from a tanker.
Tuesday *December 23*	Four square wooden plates have been recovered from the wreck of the first *HMS Invincible* which was built in 1741 and sank in the Solent in 1758.
Wednesday *December 24*	154 different species of seabirds have been seen in London this winter because of rough weather at sea, according to the London Natural History Society.
Thursday *December 25*	A British team spend Christmas Day 6000m up on the West Ridge of Everest in temperatures of –30°C.
Friday *December 26*	A very bright fireball crosses the English Channel at 2.50am over Beachy Head and fades rapidly over Kent with sonic booms and rumblings.
Saturday *December 27*	Hurricane force winds in Spain: the King and his family are forced down onto a football field in their helicopter.
Sunday *December 28*	The Grimsby to Louth railway, which opened in 1848, closes today. Avalanches in the French Alps
Monday *December 29*	The US space shuttle *Columbia* is moved to the launching pad at Cape Canaveral for lift-off next year. The 5km journey, code-named 'Operation Roll-out' takes 8 hours.
Tuesday *December 30*	A small round stained-glass window is stolen from Warwick Castle. The BBC holds a reception to celebrate 'The Archers'' 30th anniversary. AND NOW, THE ARCHERS
Wednesday *December 31*	The Kew Observatory in the Old Deer Park, Richmond, closes today after more than 200 years. It was built by George III in 1769 to observe the transit of Venus across the Sun.